Croc

Table of Contents

Chapter 3

Chapter 4

Introduction

Hook, loop and shape!

No, this isn't some sort of an abbreviated strategy to bait your fiancé into marriage. First you hook the poor, unsuspecting fellow, loop him into the marriage cord and then shape him to suit your taste. The male species are a lot smarter these days and it will take them lock, stock and barrel before they would even consider crawling towards the bait.

However, hook, loop and shape you certainly can do when you engage in one of the most endearing hobbies of all times – crochet. It's one of the few art forms left that you can do at your own leisurely pace, one writer calling it the perfect accompaniment to daydreaming.

It is probably while crocheting that strategies concerning your significant other will come most naturally. Because if you angle that hook properly and turn and twist it cleverly, then you might end up with the most effective bait there is.

If you're looking for versatility, crochet has it all. Shapes, colors, textures and weight all combine to produce potentially hundreds of objects that will make you smile and elicit oohs, ahhs and "I've got to have this" reactions from family and friends. Because once that yarn is defined into its final shape, a true labor of love manifests itself.

Also, crochet is not just an ordinary craft, certainly not a mere part of the bigger universe of sewing. If you have to ponder size and weight and yarn texture, crochet turns magically into a science. It has its own set of symbols and abbreviations, its own blueprints. Without knowing what they signify, we could not crochet, forcing us to lead a "threadbare" existence.

A crocheted object can keep us warm in the winter, cradle our boiling pots and pans, suspend our plants from the ceiling, protect our paper money and coins, cover the stains and scratches in our furniture, dress up the baby's cradle and make a fashion statement.

The fondness for crocheting has not waned since the early ages. Just glance at the arts and crafts section of any bookstore. Last time we checked, there were more books on crochet than there were books on the DaVinci code. And unhook the belief that crocheting is reserved for creatures who sit on rocking chairs all day.

Where have you been?

Teenagers are having fun with it. So are 30

somethings and those who are past their childbearing years.

Let's see if we can get you hooked...

Chapter 1

About Crochet

To set crochet apart from the rest of the sewing crowd, we'll make some distinctions:

Crocheting is a type of lace needlework that involves interlocking loops of a single thread, using a hooked needle.

Knitting is looping yarn or thread together by hand with long needles or by machinery which forms similar interlocking loops.

Sewing is working with a needle and thread to fasten stitches.

Quilting is stitching with lines or patterns through layers of cloth. It is usually employed in making bed covers and wall decorations.

Embroidering is making raised and ornamental designs on cloth, leather, etc with the use of a needle.

How crochet further stands out from these other forms will become apparent as we discuss its dynamics for producing fabric and its numerous by-products.

History of Crochet

A writer who tried to trace the history of crochet came to the conclusion that there is no real evidence to show the existence of crochet before the 19th century. Knitting, she said, preceded crochet by at least four centuries.

Why crochet did not show up until the 19th century could probably be explained by the fact that people at the time preferred more economical fabric-creating techniques. Crochet uses an enormous amount of thread to produce pieces of fabric which were much more economically produced by the ancient techniques of netting, sprang, nalbinding or knitting.

It was while Ireland was developing its lace industry that the US took up crocheting. It soon became a household activity that was loved by many American settlers.

While sewing was considered a function, crochet was entertainment. When America went to World War II in 1941, there was no such thing as time and innovation for fashion, so the idea was to make it "short and sweet." Crochet was therefore saved for special things like a touch of lace, a scarf or a friendly.

When the war ended, crochet was back in the limelight and women turned it into a hobby to create luxuries they desired: tablecloths, edgings for pillowcases, handkerchiefs and towels.

After the 1960's crochet was no longer a "domesticated" activity; the generations that followed transformed the craft into something more ambitious and non-traditional. All of a sudden, all kinds of finished fabrics were arriving at the scene, manifestations of the innovation fever that characterized the wealthy period that the US was experiencing. Since this time, 21st century crochet has had a different face, a new look. New types of hooks were born, and yarns multiplied in variety.

To take up crochet, it is important to know the basics which cover:

- ✓ Commonly used abbreviations
- ✓ Stitches
- ✓ Kinds of hooks
- ✓ Kinds of Yarns

Knowing the basics will enable you to come up with simple projects for you and your home. In fact, there are multiple projects you can create just by knowing the basics.

However, as you gain more confidence, chances are you'll want to learn advanced techniques so you can diversify your project portfolio. Who knows, you may want to make a living out of crochet. Your finished products will be selling so quickly that your hands and fingers will be feverishly moving about just to keep up with demand!

Language of Crochet

Let's begin with the more common abbreviations used in crocheting:

ch st - chain stitch

dc - double crochet

hdc - half-double crochet

sc - single crochet

sl st - slip stitch

trc - triple crochet

yo - yarn over

tr - treble crochet

sp - space

sk - skip

pat st - pattern stitch

There are other abbreviations you will use, but as a beginner in crochet, these are the most basic abbreviations you will need to memorize.

Before we go into the basic stitches, we'll mention the foundation chain, a key term in crocheting. Just as a house needs a solid foundation, crocheting needs a foundation as well. The foundation chain is defined as a cross-stitched row that serves as the base of your crocheting. It holds all your stitches and all the succeeding rows you will make.

Basic Stitches

Single Crochet – this is the first of the basic stitches. It is the shortest stitch and results in a firm, flat product. To make a single crochet, make sure the front side of the chain is facing you, then insert the hook through a chain, yarn over, pull the loop through the chain, yarn over again, and pull through both loops on the hook.

Double Crochet – as in single crochet, pass the hook from the front to the back of the work through the upper loop of a stitch of the previous row. The thread is caught on the hook and drawn through this loop.

Half-Double Crochet – a cross between a single crochet and a double crochet stitch. Begin with a yarn over, insert the hook into a stitch, yarn over and pull through the stitch; do another yarn over and pull through the three loops on your hook.

Triple Crochet – the last of the basic stitches and also the tallest. To make a triple crochet, yarn over the hook twice; insert the hook into the stitch, yarn over again and pull through the first of two loops (the two closest to the end point); yarn over again and pull through the next two loops. Yarn over one last time and pull through the remaining two loops.

Crochet Hooks

Hooks come in various sizes, shapes and the material they're made of. There are also the small steel hooks which are used with very fine cotton yarns. Aluminum and steel hooks sometimes are manufactured with plastic handles for a better grip (called "soft touch" handles). These plastic handles also put less pressure on the fingers. One thing to be cautious about is that there appear to be no standard hook sizes among manufacturers. The points and throats of different brands of hooks come in different shapes and these shapes affect the size of stitch they produce.

Parts of a Hook: a crochet hook is made up of four parts – point, throat, thumb rest and shank. The point goes into the stitch on the crocheted fabric; the throat catches the yarn. Note that the throat has to be sized accordingly in proportion to the yarn being used.

The shank holds the loops that you're working with, and is the part of the hook that determines stitch size. Finally, the thumb rest is an area where you rest your thumb to help you turn the hook easily while working.

Going from smallest to largest, aluminum or plastic hooks go from size B to Q – 2.50 mm to 15.00 mm (US), and size 14 to 2 – 2.00 mm to 7.00 mm (British).[7] One good thing to bear in mind is that the size of your yarn dictates your hook size.

Crochet Yarns

There is a slight confusion regarding yarn sizes, but don't let that discourage you. One system classifies yarn into five categories based on the approximate diameter of the yarn:

Size A – light or fine weight yarns. Ideal for thin socks and light baby clothes.

Size B – sport or medium-weight yarns. Good for indoor sweaters, baby things, dresses and suits.

Size C – worsted weight or knitting yarns – good for outdoor sweaters, hats, mittens, afghans and slippers.

Size D – bulky yarns – ideal for rugs, heavy jackets and crafts,

Size E – extra bulky – mostly used for rugs.

The other system classifies yarn based on the number of stitches per 4-inch swatch of knitting stockinette stitch:

- Fine = 29-32 sts
- Light = 25-28 sts
- Medium = 21-24 sts
- Medium-heavy = 17-20 sts
- Bulky = 13-16 sts
- Extra-Bulky = 9-12 sts

Pay special attention to gauge, an indispensable component of crochet. It can make or break your project. Correct size of the project depends on gauge. Gauge depends on the hook size, yarn size and the mood you're in that day.

When working with a pattern, the hook size is usually recommended, although you can choose to work more tightly or loosely than what the pattern suggests, but you need to work at exactly the gauge the pattern requires in order to reproduce the work accurately.

Gauge has two parts: stitch gauge and row gauge. Stitch gauge is the number of stitches in a given length of a row; row gauge is the height of the number of rows. Don't be tempted to skip the gauge swatch. Keep making swatches until your stitch gauge is correct; if you need to change hooks to make the right gauge, do so.

Chapter 2

Tools and Materials

Many crochet instructors will say that all you need to get started are your hook and ball of yarn, but you really need more than these. We gave you the parts of a hook and the different sizes, but we'll get into more detail here, as it is the "star" tool of any crocheting project. If there were no hooks, there would be no crochet.

Hooks

We've already mentioned that sizes of hooks vary from thin to thick. The thin steel hooks are used with fine cotton yarn, but the bigger ones are used for heavy wools and synthetic fibers.

Hooks are made of steel, aluminum, bone or plastic.

When doing a project from a pattern, the one who wrote the pattern will suggest a hook size, but you should be a better judge of what hook to use. Use the one you're most comfortable with and the one that will help you achieve the correct gauge for a pattern.

As you go along with your work, you may have to change hooks more than once. The essential thing when choosing a hook brand is to go with the one you work well with and that feels good on your hand. Crocheting enthusiasts buy their hooks based on the following factors: hand size, finger length, weight of the hook, and preference for aluminum or plastic.

There is no fixed formula for choosing the ideal size hook. Remember that crocheters are different. Some like to crochet tightly, some loosely, so that this makes it difficult to determine a formula. Use gauge as the key consideration – how many stitches you need to do to make an inch.

As the experts say, practice makes perfect. Experimenting is even better. If you're using a plastic hook for a particular project and you're having problems, switch over to an aluminum hook and see how that feels. In time, you'll pick your favorites and know which sizes or types give you the best results with the best feel.

Afghan Hook

You may have heard of the Afghan hook which is used for specialized crochet projects. The Afghan hook was devised so that you can hold many stitches on the hook simultaneously. If the average length of a hook is six inches, this does not give you much space. The Afghan hook was invented to make your life easier. It is much longer than your regular crochet hook and come in three lengths: 9-inch, 14-inch and 20-inch. It also has knobs at the ends to keep stitches from falling off. And thanks to clever inventors, you can find some Afghan hooks that have long, flexible cords on one end. These cords are to hold additional stitches so you can rest your work on your lap without the need to worry.

More About Yarns!

Regarding yarns, they are produced by spinning different types of fibers together. Some are natural fibers taken from plants and animals like cotton or wool; others are synthetic, such as nylon or acrylic. The yarn industry has mixed and matched fibers together to come up with a variety of sizes and textures to satisfy the demands of sophisticated crocheters. Generally, for a beginner, the easiest yarn to work with is one with a smooth surface and a medium or tight twist.

Yarns are sold by weight rather than by length. They are usually packaged into balls. The most common ball size is 1-3/4 oz (50 g) and the length of each yarn will vary depending on the thickness and fiber composition.

Wool is a good yarn to crochet with because it is stretchable, making it easy to push the point of the hook into each stitch. Silk yarn is another that is good for crocheting, but has less resilience than wool and is much more expensive.

Synthetic fiber yarns on the other hand like acrylic, nylon, and polyester are manufactured from coal and petroleum products, often made to resemble fibers. Yarns made entirely of synthetic fibers are less expensive and their benefits include stability, washing machine-safety and non-shrinkage. The only disadvantage is they tend to lose their shape when exposed to heat. A better alternative would be to buy yarn which is part synthetic, part natural fiber.

While there are common types of yarns based on weight, numerous manufacturers in numerous countries will produce yarns that don't fall within the common weight parameters of yarn. Here are the most familiar ones that are sold:

- ✓ extra-bulky,
- ✓ bulky,
- ✓ aran wool,

- ✓ worsted,
- ✓ sport,
- ✓ aran cotton,
- ✓ double knitting,
- ✓ sport mercerized cotton,
- ✓ worsted acrylic
- ✓ viscose rayon,
- ✓ linen/viscose,
- ✓ metallic viscose,
- ✓ metallic.

While we said hook and yarn are all you need to begin crochet, there are other tools that will help you considerably in making your work easier and more efficient. Here are the "extras" you'll want to keep handy.

Markers

Split rings or shaped loops made of colorful plastic would mark those places in your work if you're working with a pattern; they indicate the beginning of a row and help in counting the stitches on the foundation chain;

Tapestry Needles

These are instruments with blunt points and long eyes, and are typically used in embroidery. They vary in size and used to weave yarn ends and for sewing crochet pieces together. You may also want to have a selection of needles with sharp points for applying crochet braid, edging or borders.

Pins

For blocking tasks, the best pins are those that have a glass head and are rustproof. Plastic or pearl headed pins are good for pinning crochet.

Quilters' long pins are also ideal for pinning pieces of crochet together as the heads are clearly visible and won't slip through the crochet fabric.

Tape Measure

Choose a tape measure that has both inches and centimeters on the same side. Over time, tape measures tend to stretch so they need to be replaced to achieve measurement accuracy. A plastic or metal ruler (12 inches/30 cm) is also a good idea to measure gauge swatches.

Row Counter

This will help you keep track of the number of rows you have crocheted so far; others prefer a notebook and pencil.

Sharp scissors – small, pointed ones are good for trimming yarn and yarn ends.

Plastic Rings

These serve as foundations for making buttons. Metals rings for button foundations are not recommended because they could rust when the garment is washed.

Metal Hook Gauge

This is the only tool that will tell you the size of your hook. Don't rely on the size stamped on the hook and always check the size of your hook with a metal gauge.

Bobbins

These can hold small quantities of yarns. They're a great help when doing multi-colored work.

Store your yarns in a safe place where they won't get stained. A large, clean pillowcase might serve this purpose. When not in use, bundle your hooks together with a string or rubber band and keep them in case like a cosmetic bag or a sturdy box.

Chapter 3

Basic Techniques

Proper techniques begin with how to hold hook and yarn correctly so that you're comfortable with them when working on a project. Let's begin with holding the hook. There are two ways to hold your hook:

- Hold it as though you were holding a pencil – position and apply a light grip on the hook, or
- Hold it the same way as you would grip a spoon when mixing something thick.
- Now the yarn: a basic technique is to make a slip knot, attaching the yarn to your hook. Three simple steps to tie the slipknot:

- Loop the yarn around your left index finger
- Let the yarn slip from your finger, holding the loop between your thumb and index finger,
- With the hook held by your right hand, draw the loop up and around the hook.

Then pull each of the ends gently in opposite directions. This will tighten the knot and make it smaller.

Practice, Practice, Practice!

The technique of feeding yarn into your work takes a bit of practice. With your left hand, pick up the yarn, and with the palm of your left hand facing up, thread the yarn through the fingers. Practice holding the yarn so that it "flows" naturally through your fingers. Move your index finger up and down to increase or decrease the tightness of the yarn. As you progress, you will feel a rhythm that works best for you, making the movement more natural and effortless.

Catching the Yarn Technique

This is known as a yarn over (abbreviation: yo). Your index finger plays a crucial role in yarn over movements. Each time you catch the hook, you guide the yarn by moving your index finger up and down. To do a yarn over:

- Pass the hook under and over the yarn from back to front
- If you're having problems wrapping the yarn around all your fingers: instead of wrapping the yarn, just let it flow behind your index finger, in front of your middle and ring fingers and back behind your little finger.

Chain Stitch Technique (cs)

Going counterclockwise, loop the yarn over the hook (or else you can hold the yarn still and adjust the hook accordingly). Draw the yarn through to form a new loop without tightening the previous one. Repeat the same steps as many times as you need to make chains as specified in the pattern. A good point to remember when counting chains correctly is not to count the first slip loop as a chain. To count them afterwards, make sure they are not twisted and you are looking at the front; then count back, but don't include the loop that's still on the hook.

Single Crochet (sc):

- Insert the hook into the work (or second chain from hook), wrap the yarn over the hook and draw the yarn through the work only.
- Wrap the yarn again and draw it through both loops. You just made 1 sc.

Half Double (hdc) Technique

- Wrap the yarn over the hook and insert the hook into the work (or third chain from hook);
- Wrap the yarn over the hook, draw through the work only and wrap the yarn again;
- Draw through all 3 loops on the hook.

Double Crochet Technique

- Wrap the yarn over the hook and insert the hook into the work (for 4th chain from hook);
- Wrap the yarn over the hook, draw through the work only and wrap the yarn again;
- Draw through the first 2 loops only and wrap the yarn again;
- Draw through the last 2 loops on the hook.

- Treble Crochet Technique (tr)
- Wrap the yarn over the hook twice and insert the hook into the work (for 5th chain from hook);
- Wrap the yarn over the hook, draw through the work and wrap again;
- Draw through the first 2 loops only and wrap the yarn again;
- Draw through the next 2 loops only and wrap the yarn again; draw through the last 2 loops.

Turning Chains

This is where your foundation chain ends and you have to add rows above it. To prepare for making a new row, you make turning chains. When you get to the end of a row, you need to determine how tall your successive rows should be, and this entails crocheting a certain number of chain stitches to bring your work to the desired height of the next row. Note that the taller the stitch, the greater the number of extra chains you have to make.

Here is the number of turning chains you'll need for each stitch:

- Slip stitch = 1 turning chain
- Single crochet = 1
- Half-double crochet = 2
- Double crochet = 3
- Triple crochet = 4
- The Button Stitch

There is also what is called the bullion stitch (and bullion stitch bars). To do this, make sure the hook is thicker toward the handle and thinner toward the point than those used for other kinds of crochet.

To make an ordinary bullion stitch, your foundation chain has to be loose. Wind the yarn evenly several times around the hook; pass the hook through one stitch of the chain, 1 over is made and drawn through the loop, then another over is made, which is drawn through all the loops on the hook.

Bullion stitch bars are made the same way, the yarn is wrapped at least 10 or 12 times around the hook, and the over is drawn through all the loops except the last 2, which are joined by 1 fresh over. Hold the twists of the yarn firmly between the thumb and forefinger to make it easier to draw the hook through.

Cluster Stitch

(also called pineapple stitch)

This is used as an insertion between rows of double crochet.

- Make 1 over, insert hook under 1 stitch of the preceding row, make 1 over and draw it through as a loop;
- Make another over, insert the hook a second time under the same stitch and draw it through with another loop;

- Make a 3rd over, insert the hook a 3rd time under the same stitch and draw 1 loop through;
- Make a 4th over, insert the hook again and draw another loop through, make another over and draw the hook through the first 8 loops on the hook;
- Make another over and draw it through the last 2 loops, 1 chain, miss 1 stitch of the preceding row, and repeat all steps.

Persian Stitch

Instead of a loose, flat thread, use either one of the following to practice this technique: thick, firm thread like DMC 6 cord crochet cotton, DMC special quality crochet cotton (nos. 1 to 10), DMC knotting cotton (nos. 10 to 30), or DMC flax thread for knitting and crochet nos. 3 to 12.

This stitch is worked on from the right side only:

- Draw 1 loop through on each side of a stitch of the previous row so that there are 3 loops on the hook, including the one made by the last stitch;
- Make 1 over and pass it through all 3 loops;
- Draw another loop through beside the left-hand arm of the stitch just made to form the right hand arm of the new stitch, and another loop through the next stitch;
- Make 1 over and draw it through all 3 loops.

If you're really into crochet and want to be successful with your projects, don't be discouraged by your first attempts. The more you work on your mistakes, the better your skills will be.

We have just provided the very basic crochet techniques in this section. Start with these until you get the hang of it. Crocheting is like tennis: the more you hit the ball "over" the court, the better your shots will be.

One's grip on the racket should feel natural and comfortable, not forced. The same is true with how you hold your hook. One expert crocheter once said, if you're stressed about something while you're crocheting, that stress will show in your work.

Maybe the yarn is too tight or you missed a few important loops or chains? Give yourself plenty of time to achieve a good comfort level.

Chapter 4

Some Great Crocheting Tips!

Like in any business undertaking, the trick is to diversify. In crochet, try not to stick to one kind of hook. If you can afford it, buy an assortment of aluminum, plastic, wood and steel. As you work on more projects, going from the simplest to the most complex, you'll encounter difficulties with certain stitches and with certain yarns.

You need not give up on that project in desperation and go on to the next project. Try changing your hooks. Say, for instance, you've been using aluminum for a sweater project. The sleeves begin to pose some problems. See if switching to a plastic or wooden hook – perhaps slightly smaller or slightly bigger – might help. Keep experimenting, you just might hit the jackpot.

Bobbins

Bobbins are small plastic devices that look identical to your bread pins, except they're larger. They are especially useful when working with many colors. Instead of handling balls of yarn, crochet from the bobbin. Wrap yarn around it before starting and this way you unwind only what you need for the next few stitches.

Always count chains from the front of the chain. You begin counting with the first complete stitch above the slip knot. When working with projects, crochet instructions will indicate how many chains to make and where to start your work on the foundation chain.

Having a snarl? This is probably because you forgot to do your turning chains. The ends of your work will look "squished" because there isn't any space to allow for rows. To fix the snarl, unwind the yarn back to the end of the preceding row and then making your turning chains. Remember, it's okay to keep unwinding yarn so you could do the stitch all over again, what isn't okay is to give up!

If you like crocheting round items like doilies and tablecloths, begin with the foundation chain joined in a ring. It is the slip stitch that joins the ring. To use a slip stitch to join a ring, insert your hook under the 2 loops of the first foundation chain, and then yo! (yarn over). Next, pull the hook through the chain and the loop on the hook. One loop remains on the hook, and you have now completed a slip stitch and made a ring.

Immediately after you take up crocheting and you browse books for future projects, you will find crochet symbols used in patterns. Crochet instructions can be:

- Written out in words, with abbreviations
- Presented as symbols
- A combination of written instructions and symbols

It's going to take awhile to know the symbols and abbreviations by heart. Symbols are generally international symbols, which means that if you a pattern from England, the symbols used will be the same symbols as those in an American pattern. And since crochet symbols are international, 9 out of 10 they are the same in other countries.

Symbols are used because they save space, and experienced crocheters find they are easier to read.

Donna Kooler says it's really up to the individual to decide if she prefers to read written instructions or interpret symbols. Her advice, however, is to have both handy, if possible. If a stitch or series of stitches is not working properly based on the written instructions, you can compare the instructions to the corresponding symbols. The error could just be typographical, so this is where having both written instructions and symbols is efficient.

As she said, "Charts and written instructions clarify each other. If written instructions don't adequately explain a point, look at the chart and vice versa. Some things are almost impossible to chart, such as cylinders, while some things are much easier to read from a chart, such as lace. Both symbols and written instructions have their advantages: used together they can answer virtually any question you may have about a stitch or pattern."

Whatever you decide to do, memorizing the abbreviations will save you time in looking them up, enabling you to concentrate more on your piecework.

When reading instructions, you will most certainly see brackets and parentheses. These serve to bunch together related information or to indicate alternate stitches. Let's take an example from Kooler's book, Encyclopedia of

Crochet:

"(sk 4 ch, 5 dc in next chain) across the row"

This instruction means that you will leave 4 chains unworked – sk here means skip, hence: skip 4 chains. In the 5th chain, you will do 5 double crochets. You repeat the entire process – that is, skipping 4 chains and then doing 5 double crochets.

Confusing?

If you're just beginning, that's perfectly understandable, but as we said earlier, practice makes perfect. And we might add: practice makes comfortable! Don't worry, when you buy any book on crochet, the first chapters will always be devoted to abbreviations and symbols. And as you buy more and more books, you won't even need to read the first chapters anymore.

When we made a recipe with a certain brand cheese one day, it tasted so good because the cheese's distinct flavor contributed to the taste. We were so pleased with how the recipe turned out, we quickly dived into the garbage can to fish out the wrapper of the cheese so we could buy the same brand next time. What's the point of this tip, you ask.

Well, the same principle applies to crochet. Keep the label of the yarn you fell in love with. If a project turned out successful, chances are you picked the right kind of yarn for it. Make a note of the brand (and size and texture as well) so you won't be scratching your head next time you go shopping for crochet supplies.

This thing called ply – you see it in toilet paper labels. It's used in yarns as well. Ply refers to the number of strands that were spun together to produce a yarn – usually two, three or four. But it does not tell you the diameter of the yarn because it can be large or small.

Some yarns are difficult to crochet with. We'll name a couple so that if a project calls for these types of yarns, you'll be prepared for potential trouble spots:

Mohair – this is a soft yarn made from the hair of the Angora goat. It is an attractive fabric but it is not easy to crochet – unless you have a very openwork pattern.

Bouclé

Bouclé – also an attractive yarn for crocheting certain types of work, but not easy to handle because it is a type of yarn that has been interspersed with tight clusters, and it has an erratic thickness.

And here are yarns that are easy to crochet with: acrylic, cotton, crêpe, nylon, tricel and wool.

Fastening Off

Fastening off: when your work is complete, or if you simply want to change the color of your yarn, cut the yarn a few inches from the work. Pull this end through the last loop on the hook and draw tightly. Darn this loose end in later.

Never allow a crocheted garment to become too dirty. Careful washing does not damage any garment, but when it is very soiled, washing it will not remove all the dirt without rubbing; it is this repeated rubbing that can damage the garment. Make sure that whatever detergent you use (soap, gel, powder, etc), it is soaked in hot water, and the diluted with cold water afterwards to reduce the temperature. Make sure the garment is covered completely in the water and detergent. Allow the detergent to remove the dirt. Do not rub, and do not bring the garment up and down from the water because this will stretch it.

When shopping for crochet materials, shop intelligently. The first rule of thumb is to find a reliable store. A good store usually has inventory from reputable manufacturers. A good store also has knowledgeable and competent sales persons on site to answer your questions or give recommendations for products and materials.

Lastly, a good store will have a generous policy of returns and exchanges. It often happens that we buy an oversupply of yarns because we overestimated our needs for a particular project. When buying yarn, check label for the dye lot number because colors can vary from one dye lot to another.

Good wool yarn can be re-used. When you no longer like a wool garment that you crocheted, don't throw it away. Rip the yarn apart and re-work it into a new piece of garment.

Think "suitability." This simply means that when we buy yarn and crochet with it, it looks great on our hands but when we wear it, it turns out a disaster. Remember that yarns have characteristics that have to be considered before starting a project. For instance, fine thread yarn is good for a Victorian type doily, but it definitely won't do for a pot holder. A soft yarn would make a lovely lace shawl, but would be wrong for a man's rugged sweater.

Working rows – you'll come across this term when you start to crochet. A row is a group of stitches crocheted from one end of the piece to the other. Rows are generally worked from right to left. Count your stitches as you work or at the end of a row. Double check your count to make sure you did not increase or decrease a stitch.

- Increase and decrease – these are terms you will also encounter when crocheting.
- Increase – adding one or more stitches. External increases are worked at the beginning or end of a row. Internal increases are worked within a row.
- Decrease – eliminate one or more stitches. Internal decreases are worked within a row. External decreases are worked at the beginning or end of a row.

Randomly Crochet

Time: late 80's – early 90's

Place: Honduras

She was a Peace Corps volunteer in that country, and we don't know the exact moment when the idea hit her. She was focused and determined – two qualities that led her to form an organized group. The group started small, but it now has a large following...and what a following it turned out to be.

An idea with a solid “foundation chain”

The movement that fired her imagination had nothing to do with the Peace Corps or a local rally in Honduras for women’s rights. Her name was Gwen Blakely Kinsler and it was while she was in Honduras that she fell in love.

With crochet…

A few writers tried to trace the history of crochet, but nothing can be established, at least prior to the 18th century. There were accounts of knitting and embroidery, but crochet and crocheters were not rallying noisily to have their position in history recorded. They were more preoccupied about creating.

Anyone knows that a talented individual can be notoriously creative with hook and yarn - just by sitting quietly in a corner, head slightly bent, fingers nimble…and maybe even daydreaming. Because crochet is a relaxing activity, once the foundation chain is made, a crocheter just continues to build rows and rows of stitches. And loops and double trebles.

Gwen Blakely Kinsler returned to America and focused on her needlework by attending meetings and seminars, but most of these were attended by people who had a fondness – and possibly a side business - in embroidering. Ms. Kinsler participated regularly because she was a faithful member, but she had something else in mind: to find people among the crowds of embroiderers who wanted to unite and form a strong core of crocheters who were proud of their craft and wanted it recognized. No doubt the camaraderie was also an incentive to band together.

1994 was Ms. Kinsler's year. Coming out of a meeting of the Chain Link Crochet Conference that August, she was ecstatic. It was decided – by unanimous vote - that the Crochet Guild of America was going to be formed. It was a precarious beginning but Kinsler and others like her worked hard to make the Guild work. It wasn't long before the DMC Thread Corporation and Monsanto offered financial assistance and sponsorships.

What began as a lonely hobby for Kinsler while she was in Honduras finally blossomed into a united force of crocheters who are on their toes (and we hope fingers) with Guild activities every month of the year. Membership is open to anyone, beginner or advanced. The Guild has chapters in about 40 out of the 52 states.

Crocheters Busy as Ever!

If you think crochet is an industry on its way out, think again. Crocheters are as busy as neuro-surgeons, organic fruit growers, and fencing champions. They also share one thing in common with writers. It has to do with the words "submission guidelines."

The efforts of Ms. Kinsler and other crocheters who went on to form different organizations and councils have not been in vain. Crochet is very much alive in America and there's a demand for patterns that perseveres to this day.

As more crochet collectives form, more newsletters and magazines – not to mention e-zines and bulletin boards and community forums – are asking crocheters to send in their patterns. According to one crochet entrepreneur, there is a sustained demand for wearable crochets and crochet projects that incorporate some beading work and knitting. Granny squares and baby merchandise are fine and still have a huge following, but the new trend seems to be veering towards wearables.

Afghans were a favourite of many, and may not be the # 1 item on a crocheter's shopping list these days, but if the afghan has a unique pattern and displays an uncommon design and non-conventional style, crocheters can still submit their afghan ideas.

This is how the submission process works: a call for submission is published, usually in crochet magazines and e-zines. A good number of these publications have a section exclusively for guidelines. The publication will state its preferences as to the kinds of patterns they're looking for. They'll say "wearables" if these are what they are targeting, and the guideline will say something like "any wearable from classic to modern to hip, as long as it's fun to wear and fun to crochet."

Competitive rates are offered, and some will even offer to have your picture and your product published. So that they don't mislead any contributors, some will add a line saying that they are currently not interested in baby clothes at the moment.

Pattern submissions are then submitted to catalogs, yarn manufacturers or to any entity in the needle trade and fabric milieu that might be interested in using the pattern.

If the guidelines state "wearables", then you'll want to increase your chances of getting published by submitting a well-researched and well-written pattern. You may need to do some research in wearable catalogs, as recommended by the Crochet Guild of America.

When you submit your pattern, you will need to check your calculations (yes, do the math!)

and compare your measurements against industry standards. You'll also want to make sure that the yarn you used for the pattern is still available in the market. As with writers, you sell your rights to the buyer, but as soon as your pattern goes out of print, the rights revert to you. There's a 99% chance they'll ask you for photographs and diagrams in a specified format.

Submitting patterns and getting paid for them are only one part of the picture.

How about annual conferences, state-to-state seminars, and attendance at trade shows where the cotton and synthetic fiber industries converge and show their latest innovations in thread and yarn?

Crochet has not been put to bed. It's a dynamic collection of people who love what they do and are proud of their creations.

Some crocheters prefer to do a solo act. Every now and then you'll spot an ad from a lone crocheter showcasing her designs and patterns and is ready to accept orders. Crocheting is a brisk business, and experienced crocheters know a good piece when they see one.

Some Crochet Innovations

It's called diversification. Indeed, crocheters know a thing or two about it. Beads are the rage in crochet these days.

Would you like a schmoo? You don't know what it is? Schmoos are mythical critters that bring joy and happiness to anyone who carries them around. With a curious variety of beads these days, you can create schmoos and personalize them.

Or, has anyone heard of Clover's new hairpin lace tool? Or lariats that are made with cut pearl beads? There's one crocheter on cyberspace who talks her own language, and she's having a lot of fun. That's the wholesome quality of crochet. People like her make you wish you had pursued that grade school crochet course you took. Maybe we should have watched grandma more closely when her agile fingers tackled hook and yarn. Crocheters live in their own universe, and judging from what we've read so far, it is a happy universe.

We read a primer on bead crochet ropes recently, and it is fascinating. It was a step-by-step procedure for working with bead ropes for crocheting and yarn overs and thread sizes. The writer was sharing her bead rope savvy and explained her tips and tricks on how to pull the thread and how to get the first line of beads into the thread.

Freeform crocheting is another innovation. What is it exactly?

We compare it to a kind of experimental cuisine with no set recipe. In freeform crochet, we work without a pattern. It goes something like this: take a crumbly piece of yarn, do some stitches until it takes form, then attach it to another crochet piece of a different color, fasten the two pieces together, then put in a stitch on top, another one below, and now add a motif...another stitch here, there, time for a yarn over, make rows, throw in a bead maybe.

What did you end up with? You bet it's something that's definitely worth showing in a freeform crochet forum or ezine. Even crazy shapes built out of nothing have a place in the crochet world. That's why it's called freeform. Anything goes - sky's the limit - disco dancing minus the dance instructor.

Freeform, according to one crocheter, is like painting. It can be born out of an abstract idea or a realist one. It can be 2-D or 3-D; whatever it is, it is always beautiful. Like love, it is never planned, it just happens.

Spread the Word; Share Your Love

The Craft Yarn Council of America initiated a brilliant idea. Using the motto, "Each One Teach Two" it is encouraging all teachers nationwide to teach students six years old and older how to crochet. The Craft Yarn Council provides the lesson plans and tells teachers what they can teach beginners, given that starting a chain is probably one of the hardest techniques to master.

Students are asked to use a larger hook – the H or I aluminum hook – since these hooks will give them a better grip on correct tension. Most beginners tend to crochet too tightly, the Council says. The idea is to establish a “chain” of crocheters; each person teaches two other people, and those two people will teach two others. The goal is to have everyone – well almost everyone – crocheting.

Teachers don’t have to be experts as the instructions are clearly spelled out. Instruction sheets can be downloaded from the Council’s web site and certificates are awarded at the end of the lessons.

If you think about this initiative, it dawns on you that the Yarn Council of America is making a last-ditch effort to save the yarn industry. The more there are crocheters and knitters in the US, the more there will be demand for yarn and other supplies. It’s a tested method to keep any particular segment of American business to stay afloat.

But then again…

We hardly think the yarn industry is faltering in any way. Evidence suggests it is thriving and doing very well. If crochet and knit managed to make it to the present century, that means that the needle trade has nothing to fret about. Knitting and crocheting are mainstays of a country's clothing endeavors, and as long as people continue using their creative bent, then hook and yarn will be in constant supply. And even if the hobby was pushed towards oblivion, people all over the world will still need sweaters and mitts and pompom hats. Who's going to make them?

Going back to the Yarn Council of America, their campaign does have merit even if the commercial motive is blatantly visible. First, by urging teachers to engage their students in a few minutes of crochet each day, these youngsters will have something to keep their hands busy.

If it's one more efficient way of keeping them out of the streets and away from drugs, the Yarn Council just killed two birds with one stone. They promote the interests of the yarn industry, and they keep children safe at home. Instead of poking needles into their arms, they simply take up the hook and loop threads and create a piece they can use or turn into an entrepreneurial hobby.

There is something uplifting about the blissful "I made it myself!"

We know of many career women and housewives who are experts at a craft and somehow, wearing what they make – be it a crocheted scarf, a beaded pendant, a knitted mitten – elicits admiration and "would you consider making one for me, I'll pay you" type of question. In fact one woman we once knew at work wore a bracelet and necklace set that she had made from some Japanese glass beads and that same day, she left work with $400.00 worth of orders. She didn't expect that to happen, and she never thought that it could turn out to be a small home-based business for her. The lady now has a web site and can't keep up with orders from people she doesn't even know who are emailing her from as far away as the Yukon.

We suspect the same is going on with crocheters who are wearing what they make, with no hidden motives. Remember how one individual remarked that there are dozens of silent millionaires all over the world?

We wonder what percentage of them are crocheters. We'll never know, will we? They sit quietly at home, by the fireplace perhaps, and churning out these marvelous pieces of crochet that will simply be added to an inventory with rapid turnover. Silent waters run deep. The wealth of a nation lies in the nooks and crannies of every home – suburban and rural.

Our Wall Street types can hustle all they want – they can blow their horns about how many mergers and acquisitions they've accomplished in a 45-day period, but you know something?

There are crocheters who are making much, much more.

Kudos to the Yarn Council of America. It's helping America sell thread – a noble mission no doubt. That way, no child, woman or man needs to ever live a threadbare existence. At least everyone will be adequately clothed. Whether they have adequate food and shelter remains to be seen. So far so good, though. Ninety nine percent of world efforts are geared towards salvaging the human race.

Who? Martha Stewart?

And who has not heard of Martha Stewart? She was that lady that turned dinnerware and table clothes into a billion dollar industry. But let's leave that to the business analysts to dissect – this whole affair about how much money she made and the insider trading and whatever other felony crime she was charged with.

But let's lighten up here. When she left federal prison, Martha Stewart was reported to be wearing a poncho that was crocheted by a friend in prison. You guessed right! Martha Stewart managed to steer away attention from the facial worry lines she earned in prison to the poncho!

That poncho hugged the headlines – at least in Omnimedia and bulletin boards of crochet community forums. Interpretations of the poncho pattern have been circulated widely, but we can't ascertain whether the original one was ever traced back to the creator. One crochet designer – Lily Chin – tried to replicate it and wore her version on the CBS Morning Show. She called it...the Freedom Poncho (what else?).

We'll put on our crocheted thinking cap on and analyze this poncho item more closely:

Famous celebrity Martha Stewart wears a crocheted poncho while leaving prison

The poncho was crocheted by an inmate

Did the inmate learn crochet while in prison or was she already crocheting before incarcerated?

Why would prison authorities give an inmate a hook that she could turn into a weapon?

We think the last two points are revealing. Sadly, they only reveal our idiotic misperceptions and our urban neurosis. We need to broaden our minds a bit, get some fresh air so we can think like poetic thinkers do. A wholesome way of thinking is the better alternative.

Isn't it wonderful that people in prison can be given something to do so that they too can be productive citizens like the rest of us outside bars?

Many of us who are free merely meander our existence away, a steep price to pay for freedom. Is there something about prison life that turns people into contemplative beings, where they end up realizing that working with one's hands can be one of the best therapies in the world?

It shouldn't be a case of "let them eat cake". Why not take the Yarn Council of America to task and tell them, "let them learn crochet?" A poet once said that it's not the destination that counts, it's the journey. In crochet, it's not the poncho that counts, but each of the creative strokes that form together into a cohesive and beautiful whole. Nothing too tight, nothing too footloose and fancy free.

This is what crocheting means. It's a compromise between two extremes, a coming together of one row, one chain, one single stitch, and two double loops. Crochet is like life slowly coming to be. And when it does, it comes in vibrant colors and amazing swatches. It becomes a source of pride for the maker, and a source of genuine desire on the part of others to imitate. Life imitating life.

Well, maybe we've stretched that thought too far. But do think about it. Drugs and prostitution eventually destroy human minds. Crocheting can save them.

Shed off all perceptions about crocheting being an older lady's craft. Not by a mile. Citing a study done by Research Inc. in Atlanta, Cindy Wolff said there are about 38 million women in the United States who know how to knit or crochet. In 1994, that number was 34.7. Those who learn to crochet and join the fold are usually women under 35. We've got Hollywood celebrities like Julia Roberts and Cameron Diaz to thank for sharing the limelight with the craft.

Resources A-Bounty!

It's never too late. If you're nine or tugging your 90's and your hands will let you, you can try your hand at crochet and see if you'll get hooked. Apart from the 20 or so books you can pick up at your local library, there's hundreds more in the bookstores and even on eBay.

Freebies, you ask? Of course! They're all yours to take from the World Wide Web. Start with the Yarn Council of America (craftyarncouncil.com) and the Crochet Guild of America (CGOA) at crochet.org). They'll all be waiting for you with open arms.

Be lonely no more. Even if only for the sake of camaraderie – even the online kind of camaraderie – reach out and show them what your fingers can concoct.

If you're fascinated with history, take a look at CGOA's hook classification that goes back as early as 1880. And if you happen to travel to Canada and you're cruising along the banks of the Ottawa River, the Canadian Museum of Civilization – minutes away from Ottawa – has an interesting collection of crochet hooks. The collection may be a bit slanted, because Canada is proud of its Inuit heritage, but our aboriginals could share some enlightening facts about the crochet hook with you.

Why wait? Get chained and hooked now. Yarn over. Do a double and treble stitch. And then join the club!

Conclusion

There's no legislation in any country that says men can't crochet. It's a hobby and craft that's open to anyone who is willing to try. But the majority of crocheters seem to be women, and we have yet to stumble upon a crocheting book that's written by men.

In some respects, women are fortunate creatures. They'll climb the corporate ladder like a man and fight tooth and nail to get management to notice them, or if they're made of a softer fiber, they'll take the fiber route and weave their talents in quieter and domestic activities such as knitting, quilting or crocheting.

We don't know about the knitting and quilting industries, but crochet seems to have held its own. It's many centuries old and has its own history; it hasn't folded up despite our preoccupation with – and entrapment within – our push-button lifestyles.

Somehow, crocheting survived it all. It didn't buckle down to the technological upheavals that have forced many other industries to disappear from the scene. Oh yes, the staying power of hook and yarn is apparent. They're very much alive and have not been relegated to attics collecting dust and memories. From doilies and pot holders, crochet has graduated with flying colors, coming up with its own slew of innovation styles. Just look around - how many of the objects you see have been made by the adroit fingers of a devoted crocheter?

As we said, women are fortunate creatures. When they burn out in the office and no longer want to analyze profit and loss statements or inventory lead times, they have the alternative of changing jobs or testing their entrepreneurial leanings.

Some love to cook and go on to catering, some adore jewelry and go on to bead making or gemstones (so they can specialize in creating Reiki gemstones for instance) or some take up crochet and go on to setting up boutiques or leaving their work with handicraft merchants.

Or some take up crochet for its therapeutic qualities – and only for that reason. And if it's true that crochet is conducive to daydreaming, well...why not indeed?

To get you warmed up to crochet, we encourage you to begin with simple projects – a doily for example is like lasagna. It's the first thing an individual wants to whip up as soon as she learns the rudiments of cooking. The doily must be the most basic work you can crochet. And then when you get better, you may want to do a shawl or even children's dresses.

Crochet Guide

CPSIA information can be obtained at www.ICGtesting.com
Printed in the USA
BVOW03s0410090914

366052BV00013BA/389/P

9 781496 177667